Don't Worry, You'll Get In

100 Winning Tips for Stress-Free College Admissions

**Mimi Doe
and Dr. Michele A. Hernandez**

MARLOWE & COMPANY
NEW YORK

DON'T WORRY, YOU'LL GET IN
100 Winning Tips for Stress-Free College Admissions

Copyright © 2005 Mimi Doe and Michele A. Hernandez

Published by
Marlowe & Company
An Imprint of Avalon Publishing Group Incorporated
245 West 17th Street • 11th floor
New York, NY 10011

AVALON
publishing group incorporated

Library of Congress Cataloging-in-Publication Data

Doe, Mimi.
Don't worry, you'll get in : 100 winning tips for stress-free college
admissions / Mimi Doe and Michele A. Hernandez.
p. cm.
ISBN 1-56924-367-0
1. Universities and colleges--United States--Admission--Handbooks, man-
uals, etc. I. Hernadez, Michele A. II. Title.

LB2351.2.D64 2005
378.1'61'0973--dc22

2004065558

9 8 7 6 5 4 3 2 1

Designed by Maria Elias

Printed in the United States of America

> Contents

< iii >

< iv >

> About the Authors

MIMI DOE is the award-winning author of *Nurturing Your Teenager's Soul: A Practical Approach to Raising a Kind, Honorable, Compassionate Teen; Busy but Balanced: Practical and Inspirational Ways to Create a Calmer, Closer Family; Drawing Angels Near; and 10 Principles for Spiritual Parenting: Nurturing Your Child's Soul*, which was awarded a Parents' Choice Approved Seal and was a finalist for the Books for a Better Life Award. She founded the popular Web site www.SpiritualParenting.com and holds a master's degree in education from Harvard University.

Dubbed a "parenting guru" by *Ladies Home Journal*, Mimi is the preeminent expert in the area of spiritual parenting and instilling balance and awareness in the household. She takes a practical yet deeply soulful approach to her subject, offering simple suggestions that can be integrated into the everyday lives of even the busiest families.

Mimi is featured in weekly segments on the Hallmark Channel's New Morning TV and has appeared on the *Oprah Winfrey Show* and the *CBS Early Show*. Her work has been covered in such publications as *Child, Parenting, McCall's, Family Circle, Redbook, Reader's Digest, Publishers Weekly, USA Today*, the *London Independent, Christian Science Monitor*, and the *Washington Post*.

Mimi reaches over fifty thousand parents through her online newsletter "Spiritual Parenting Thought for the Week" and through workshops and seminars worldwide. She is a featured expert on Beliefnet.com and a contributor to iVillage's parenting section, ParentSoup. Parenting groups based on Mimi's *10 Principles for Spiritual Parenting* are meeting around the world.

She lives in Concord, Massachusetts, with her husband and two teenaged daughters.

< V >

DR. MICHELE A. HERNANDEZ has come to be known as the "admissions guru" through her college consulting work with high school students and her best-selling books *A Is for Admission*, *The Middle School Years*, and *Acing the College Application*. She is one of America's leading experts in selective college admissions and counseling services and has been featured in hundreds of newspapers, magazines, and radio and television programs, including *Newsweek*, *Bloomberg*, the *New York Times*, the *Wall Street Journal*, the *New York Post*, *Atlantic Monthly*, the *Today Show*, *CNN*, and *MSNBC*. Her online newsletter at hernandezcollegeconsulting.com has a growing following.

As an assistant director of admissions at Dartmouth College for four years and the academic dean of a private high school in South Florida, Michele has crafted a unique angle for assisting students in gaining admission to the most selective colleges, incorporating her "inside perspective" on the admissions adventure. She graduated Phi Beta Kappa from Dartmouth College in 1989 and went on to earn a master's degree in English and comparative literature from Columbia University and a doctorate in education. In her spare time, Michele reads as many books as she can, stargazes, exercises, and hangs out with her family. She is married to Bruce Bayliss, who is head of a private school in Portland, Oregon, and has two young children and two golden retrievers. They live in Lake Oswego, Oregon.

To contact the authors, head over to:
www.DontWorryGetIn.com

There you will find updates to the tips and ideas presented in this book as well as lots of other goodies.

< vi >

> Introduction

When Mimi and I first met, it was like a cosmic blast
with sparks flying and jet-stream bursts streaming in all
directions. And this was only over the phone! She called
to interview me for a book project about parenting she
was working on at the time, but after an hour-long
chat, I doubt either of us remembered the reason for
the original call. Between her expertise on parenting
and mine on college admissions, we could not stop gen-
erating ideas and advice. I am just about the fastest
talker on earth to begin with, but I can tell you that by
the end of the hour, I was talking faster than usual and
Mimi was spouting more ideas per minute than I could
keep up with. We knew then it was the beginning of a
beautiful friendship.

Over the next year or so, we spoke on an almost daily
basis, exchanging advice about our own kids (Mimi's
are older, in high school heading toward college, and
mine are younger, twenty-one months and elementary
school), how to handle the stress of college admissions,
and how to keep our collective cools during all the
stressful times that invade any family where kids are
present. It was out of these conversations that the idea
for this book was born: why not combine Mimi's
expertise in parenting with mine in college admissions?
No one had ever written a college admissions guide
that addressed the emotional side of college admissions, arguably one of the most stressful processes

< vii >

families go through. I've been doing private college admissions counseling for the past seven years, and at the end of the process, parents always surprise me by thanking me for saving the family rather than for helping their child get into a particular college (although they get to that eventually).

Mimi and I realized that families have to be armed with as much information as possible. A well-planned college journey is much less stressful than a haphazard one thrown together on an ad hoc basis. Timing is everything, and super-informed parents and students will always be more prepared and less stressed out than those who have not done their research. But sometimes families acquire all the "hard facts" without planning for the emotional backlash. That is where our book comes in. We have organized it in a way that is as user-friendly as possible. There are ten chapters that cover the ten most important aspects of the college admissions process. Within each chapter, on the left-hand page, ten tips are provided that are geared toward the hard facts, the knowledge you need to succeed. I wrote these pages to highlight the most important information for parents and students to keep in mind. On the right-hand page are strategies and advice for how to successfully approach college admissions without giving up your soul, elevating your stress level, or giving in to the urge to throw yourself off a tall bridge. Of course, Mimi wrote all the right-page tips!

Successful students and parents realize that part of getting through this sometimes horrible and

< viii >

seemingly heartless process is to maintain a sense of inner equilibrium and calm while attending to all the details. This book provides an easy blueprint to do just that! Best of luck, and let us know if we've helped you in your college journey as a family and if at the end of the day, your family isn't closer to each other than ever before.

—Michele Hernandez

Michele told you how we met and why we wanted to offer you the tools in this book. I think they are actually one and the same. Some sort of synergy brought Michele and me together so we could help you get into the college that's your perfect match without a lot of stress and angst. Both of us love teenagers and believe you have the power to change the world. We've given you specific ways to focus your energy and vitality to move through this chapter of your life with grace and joy rather than with frantic stress and exhaustion. Many of the hundreds of teenagers I have talked to and worked with are unable to be fully in the moment to enjoy their high school years, because they are so busy worrying about how each action they take will affect their college choices. Relax! Don't relax *too* much, but do let go of that obnoxious inner voice that constantly judges you as to whether or not you stack up. Although none of us can control everything that happens, we can influence the outcome more often than we think. Feeling helpless in the face of stress is the real enemy,

< ix >

not the stress itself. Go through *Don't Worry, You'll Get In* slowly and see what resonates. Don't feel you have to read it straight through, but rather take it tip by tip as they apply to your stage in the admission process. Use the book as you would a private coach who is there just for you. It's us, Michele and Mimi, shouting "YOU CAN DO IT" in each tip you read. It's us, Michele and Mimi, reminding you to stay organized and wear your pj's to the SAT tests if that's what will make you feel calm. We won't take it too hard when you throw this book across the floor and swear at us as you edit yet another draft of yet another essay because we told you so. We won't go away—we'll just shout a bit louder, YOU CAN DO IT!

I believe in divine order—things unfold as they are meant to. That doesn't mean you can sit around eating tofu and meditating all day. You have to do the legwork and rise to meet the challenges in life. But you have the guidance you need always at the ready. The important thing is not to lose all perspective. Sure, for college admissions it's us talking to you through this book and making the admission process more transparent, but it's also inside of you, that still small voice or gut feeling that you can count on for most decisions. That's your always-available source. Tune in to it often during this time. Trust yourself. And most of all, have fun! Life is really good and so are you! Let us hear from you so we can stop all that shouting!

—Mimi Doe

< X >

One

Your High School Academic Record

> Achieve Your Best

The capacity of man himself is only revealed when, under stress and responsibility, he breaks through his educational shell, and he may then be a splendid surprise to himself no less than to his teachers.

—Harvey Cushing, U.S. surgeon

> Get to know your teachers

One of the most important parts of the college admissions process is the strength of your teacher recommendations. Colleges take these very seriously, as they help sort out who is a high-impact, straight-A student versus a low-impact, straight-A student. Take the time to get to know your teachers during your high school years. Speak to them after class, ask questions, do extra work, and don't let yourself be an anonymous presence in class. Be the student you would love to have in class if you were the teacher!

< 2 >

> Embrace Learning with Gusto

Obstacles cannot crush me, every obstacle yields to stern resolve.

—Leonardo da Vinci, artist

> Open your awareness to the other people in your life

The teachers around you, for instance, offer an endless source of information. All you have to do is ask. But make sure you aren't focused only on what you want out of the relationship. Teachers know the difference between a "schmoozer" and a student who is truly eager to learn and contribute. When you shift from being self-absorbed to caring about others and making meaningful connections, you will find a support system.

< 3 >

> Go the extra mile

Colleges want to see how you've gone above and beyond what is required. If summer reading requires reading a book, read some essays or criticism about the book. Do extra work on a research paper, read beyond what's required in class, bring in outside material as a resource. Show your teacher that you're pushing yourself and your intellectual explorations. Don't settle for your second-best effort. Share with your teachers the books you've loved, articles from the newspaper, or any "outside" information that is relevant to your class. While you don't want to brownnose, you do want to show your teacher that you can relate outside materials to what you are studying in class.

Above and beyond

< 4 >

> Take charge of your academic life

Don't leave your course selections up to someone else. Map out your high school course load and reach for the stars. Sure you want to take the advice of your teachers, counselors, and parents, but ultimately you are the one who is driving this process, so be thoughtful in your approach. Remain honest with yourself in the process. Are you typically afraid of risk? If so, pushing yourself to take all honors classes may put you over the edge. On the other hand, moving gently out of your comfort zone and accepting the challenge may allow you to grow and succeed beyond what you believe is possible. Don't allow fear of failure to hold you back from experiences that will raise the bar.

Take charge

< 5 >

> Use your guidance counselor as a resource

Your guidance/college counselor provides an important piece of the puzzle for college admissions officers. They are the "voice" of your school, summarizing how you stack up next to your classmates in the academic competition. They are also your official advocates throughout the college admissions process, even if you use an outside counselor. It's never too early to set up an appointment to introduce yourself and to keep your counselor updated on your latest accomplishments. Prepare a short summary of all your extracurricular and academic accomplishments, especially if they took place outside of school. How else will your counselor find out the necessary information to support you? College counselors are your strongest allies besides teachers, so use them to your advantage throughout your four years of high school!

use your allies

< 6 >

> Carve out an appointment with yourself at the beginning of each semester and/or when you are feeling overwhelmed

When you have too much to do, find some time in your day to sit down and plan—doing so will prevent future problems. One busy sixteen-year-old confessed that she hid in the bathroom to find some uninterrupted minutes. Even ten minutes of planning can save hours of doing. Take an even larger chunk of time to schedule a meeting with yourself. Evaluate your life. I know it sounds overwhelming, but taking some time to pause and assess what your interests are academically, for instance, will help guide you in your class decisions for next year. If you discover in your assessment that you truly hate studying languages but feel you "should" keep pressing onward in that area, you may be causing yourself unnecessary stress. Meet with your guidance counselor or another mentor and share your findings. Perhaps his or her input will help guide you to the right choices.

sit down and plan

< 7 >

> Challenge yourself with tough classes

Did you know colleges rate the rigor of your course load? They rely upon guidance counselors to rate your course load on a 1 to 4 scale, with 4 being the most rigorous. You are judged by the standard at your school, so make sure if the "norm" is three Advanced Placement (AP) classes during senior year, you at least meet that or go beyond. Remember, an A average or top rank in class is undermined by a weak course load. Rank is always looked at along with course rigor.

challenge yourself

< 8 >

> Pay attention to stress alarms

When stress builds in a particular class—as exams approach or you're running into a brick wall in your research—postpone other important decisions and resist new demands. Turn inward and focus on your highest priorities. If you allow your mind to dwell on the entire spectrum of what you have to accomplish, you could go mad; instead, rein in your thoughts and focus on the task at hand.

Turn inward

< 9 >

> Don't fill your schedule with fluff

Colleges weigh your high school transcript very
highly and scrutinize your course selections.
Therefore, it does not look good to take wood-
shop, band, and basket weaving while your classmates are pushing themselves. Some high
schools even weight top classes, so you end up
being punished for taking "easy" classes because
your rank will drop. As an additional challenge,
take six academic courses rather than the tradi-
tional five—add an extra language or history
course.

Push yourself

< 10 >

> Refuse to do anything that violates your personal values

Remain clear on what truly matters to you. If your friend is in crisis but you've got a Spanish test—follow your inner compass. Get your friend the help she needs and talk to your Spanish teacher about the possibility of a day's delay in taking the test. Or if something looks as if it might be on the verge of being unethical, assume it is. Stress comes when you go against your inner sense of true right and wrong.

follow your
inner compass

< 11 >

> Pursue learning outside the classroom

Your high school doesn't offer philosophy? Check your local community college, nearby college campus, or online courses. Colleges are impressed by students who take their love of learning beyond the bounds of the high school classroom. Do your homework—investigate the options in your town and beyond. Don't just rest on your laurels and say there were no other opportunities—make your own!

Make your own opportunities

< 12 >

> Reach out and help others

Sometimes we just need to "get over ourselves." Consider tutoring kids in lower grades or acting as a mentor for someone without the resources you have. Do you love American history, for instance? Take your passion and share it with others. Lead an afternoon course at your town's middle school, or start a history book club for elders in your community. As you give of yourself, you will receive benefits you never dreamed of.

help others

< 13 >

> Plan ahead

Toward the beginning of high school, look at
some examples of academic activities that top
students have pursued, and project yourself forward four years (*Acing the College Application* has
many examples). Aim to achieve your potential
in your main areas of expertise—enter competitions, compete with others outside of your
narrow sphere of high school. Colleges are
impressed when candidates stand out on the
regional, state, or national level in academic
activities like Olympiads, Quiz Bowl, national
math exams, debate, and so on.

project yourself
forward

< 14 >

> Articulate your goals

Begin the habit of writing down your goals, and watch your dreams come true. Write down your goals for the next month, six months, and four years. The trick here, however, is to write them in a positive voice. So rather than saying "I want to get good grades," say, "I am now on the honor roll, doing my best ever in school and am happily watching those A's come in."

Write it down

< 15 >

> Seek help when you need it

Don't wait until you're failing a class to get help!
If you need extra assistance to succeed in a class,
be sure to look into getting a tutor. Often the
best tutors are students in that class or someone
in the next grade who has had your same
teacher. If you use a student, you'll pay less and
you'll get inside knowledge about that particular
teacher. In certain cases you'll want to rely on a
professional tutor.

Seek help to succeed

< 16 >

> Create a team of supporters

Think of three or four people who can help you with specific goals (improve your confidence, critique your photography, join you on your Saturday runs, help you deepen your knowledge for an AP exam, etc.). Be bold and reach out to these people. It's an honor to be asked, and you may be surprised at how a team of supporters can infuse your goals with the power to manifest.

Reach out for support

< 17 >

> Keep a strict time schedule

Strong students are always experts in time management. Be sure to track all your short-term and long-term academic projects so you can make the most of your limited time. Keep a daily planner or computer spreadsheet to help you stay on top of your increasingly difficult workload.

Manage your time well

< 18 >

> Take charge of your life by controlling who and what is surrounding you

Think of your life as a glass jar. There's only so much "stuff" that will fit into that fragile jar. If you fill it with the wrong things—brainless distractions that keep you from focusing on studying and moving forward—and the wrong people—negative folks who only wear you down—you won't have time for positive experiences and supportive people. Wrong choices add up and cause your jar to become way too full, and stress is the result. The right people and positive experiences bring happiness and success. Make a conscious choice about who and what take your time and attention.

Be selective

< 19 >

> Outline what you have read as the class progresses

Top students take advantage of academic breaks to catch up on work and then to stay a week ahead. Do some prereading: read the next novel or the next few chapters in your textbooks so you know where the teacher is going. Reread what you have covered in class and outline the chapters in your notebook so you can review throughout the school year, not just at the end of the year. Impress your teachers with your grasp of what's coming up and what has gone by, and bring in outside sources that relate.

Stay ahead

< 20 >

> Understand your personal learning style

Figure out how you are best able to retain information. Do you like to hear it, see it, or write it?
Maybe a combination of all three? How about
studying? Are you freshest first thing in the
morning? If so, than schedule study times
accordingly. Do you like to create rewards for
yourself in order to complete sections of your
studying? Then do so. Are group study sessions
just the trick for you? Whatever works for your
learning style is key. There's no magic formula or
one-size-fits-all for school success.

Know your style

< 21 >

Two
Extracurricular Involvement

> Make Your Mark

The time to relax is when you don't have time for it.

—Sydney J. Harris

> Remember less is more

Colleges would much rather see you pursue two to three interests in depth rather than seven or eight on a superficial level. Better to excel in a few areas than be mediocre in many. Don't just be a joiner—aim to take a leadership role in your major activities. Instead of being a "member" of a club where you spend twenty minutes a week, be the president or founder of a club that is more time intensive. Throw your efforts behind one or two major activities, and challenge yourself to achieve at the regional, state, or national level. Colleges will assign you an extracurricular rating just as they do an academic ranking. You'll receive a higher ranking if you truly excel in a few select areas than if you are simply a "member" of many clubs.

< 24 >

> Do What You Love and Success Will Follow

Start a huge, foolish project, like Noah. It makes absolutely no difference, what people think of you.

—Rumi, Sufi master and poet

> Combat the blues

It may sound counterintuitive, but put yourself out into the world rather than withdrawing and feeling sorry for yourself when you are down. Get involved in activities with a social aspect— clubs, teams, theater groups. Later, take time to be alone. In one study, teens admitted spending more than a quarter of their waking hours by themselves. After returning to friends and family, they felt more cheerful, alert, and involved.

EXTRACURRICULAR INVOLVEMENT

< 25 >

> Focus on a few key areas

Step back and take a serious look at your strengths. If you love music, feel free to join several different ensembles, play in competitions, perform in the pit orchestra, and continue your lessons. Colleges do not want well-rounded students—they want a well-rounded class! Be the top cello player or the top singer in your school and community.

focus

> Learn the fine art of saying "no"

Practice saying "no" when someone urges you to take on more than you can comfortably fit into your schedule. Remember, every time you say "yes" to something, you must necessarily say "no" to something else, whether you want to or not. No admissions officer wants to see a zillion activities described and a listless, burned-out kid. Be discerning and follow your heart. Learn to say "no" and mean it.

Be discerning

< 27 >

> Let your enthusiasm be contagious

Found a new activity you love? Recruit your friends to pitch in, join, or help you run a club. You'll be a much better leader if you have some friends working with you and are able to transmit your love of the activity to a group of people. Teachers and administrators at your school will take note as well. Ideally you'd like school administrators and teachers to comment on the positive effect you've had on the school environment.

enthusiasm

< 28 >

> Don't try to duplicate someone else's achievements

March to your own drummer, be true to yourself—as cliché as these sound, you will feel less stress and more joy during your high school years if you take them to heart. If it seems as though adults are trying to mold you into someone you aren't, speak up. Show them by your actions that you are following your own inner voice, and if you begin to doubt, remember that true success comes from unfolding into your true self.

be true to yourself

< 29 >

> You don't have to be an athlete

Unless you are strong enough to be a recruited athlete (and most strong athletes never even reach that level), colleges couldn't care less if you play a sport as long as you can account for your free time. Of course they want to see you pursue your interests, but if you don't like sports, don't feel that you have to force yourself to play. Pursue music, scrap booking, astronomy—whatever!

pursue your interests

< 30 >

> Strive for balance

Pressure may seem inevitable as you prepare for college admissions, but there are ways you can cope and thrive. Watch for burnout! Signs of it include frustration, deep fatigue, little patience, difficulty in sleeping and concentrating, little or no appetite, and a lack of enthusiasm for life. You can be a success, achieve great things, and remain true to yourself without running yourself ragged.

Don't burn out

< 31 >

> Examine fully all awards and programs in your field of interest

Do you like politics? Try competing in Model United Nations, national-level debate, or Presidential Classroom. If you like the classics, enter competitions for the Junior Classical League. If you don't know what awards or competitions are available in your areas of interest, ask around; your teachers may know, or you can do some research on the Internet to find out. Chances are your college counselor can steer you in the right direction.

Try competing

< 32 >

> When you do what you enjoy, you have more energy

When you go against your heartfelt desires, you drain yourself. I'm not implying you use this as an excuse for discontinuing homework, but make choices in your extracurricular life that lead you to feel happy, alive, and creative. In fact, begin a list of these "alive" times and choose more of those activities.

do what you enjoy

< 33 >

> Be a leader

Top colleges look for the top leaders, the presidents, the editors in chief, the captains. If you don't think you can rise to that level in a particular activity, focus your efforts elsewhere. You want to be the student who is noted for spurring others into action, not the one who sits on the sidelines and watches as others run with the ball. Make yourself a "high impact" applicant, someone who clearly makes a difference.

make a difference

< 34 >

> Alter your brain waves

The more you can work on your relaxation
habits, the more you are able to change
your brain waves. Yup, no kidding. And once
those brain waves are slowed down a bit, you
are better able to hear your intuitive voice,
which is your inner compass. Following this still
small voice will never fail to lead you in the right
direction. "I can't decide if I have enough time
to take a leadership position here or if I should
join x club or try out for y play." Pause . . .
become still . . . listen to your inner promptings.
Then, combine that with logic and you're all set
to move forward with the right decision.

Relax

< 35 >

> Make a name for yourself

In the case of almost every successful applicant, colleges are able to assign a "tag line" to you that sets you apart, like "Susie is the champion figure skater who started her own graphics design business." You want to make sure you present your strongest traits so colleges will remember who you are and will know how to sum you up when you're presented to admissions committees.

Set yourself apart

< 36 >

> Select activities that you love

See your extracurricular activities as a break from your stress rather than a strategy for getting into college. One teen told me: "I love sports because it's like my school is saying it's okay to do what I enjoy. I don't worry about an upcoming test while I'm on the playing field." Nurturing your passion should be a stress reliever, not a stress inducer.

Nurture your passion

< 37 >

> Be an entrepreneur

Do you like babysitting? Walking dogs? Helping others with computers? Start your own business and develop it. Many students show colleges they are "movers and shakers" by starting a small business aligned to their skills. Think about how you can turn one of your talents into a marketable skill.

Be a mover and a shaker

< 38 >

> Pick a cause you feel strongly about

Help others by taking one of your interests and turning it into a community service event. If you are great at fixing up bicycles, then set up a non-profit group that takes in old bikes, turns them around, and delivers them to homeless shelters. Is there a cause in your local community that needs attention? Raise money on their behalf by tying in the fund-raiser to your hobbies. It's particularly exciting if your event can become an ongoing community endeavor. For example, create an annual bulb sale (you buy the bulbs in bulk or get a garden store to donate them), and give the funds to community gardens that grow for local shelters. You'll find that when you are passionate about a cause, others will be happy to help.

Help others

< 39 >

> Think of the big picture

How do you want to define yourself? As the musician who also likes golf, or the scientist who also is a master chef? Envision how you want admissions officers to see you. Drop any extraneous activities, and focus on those that fill in your overall portrait of who you want to be.

define yourself

< 40 >

> You are the story

Everything you choose to become involved in—outside of your studies—paints a picture of the person you are. So be conscious about your choices and build upon your interests so that the compilation of activities represents depth and dimension rather than just a list of random clubs.

Paint a picture

< 41 >

> Keep a list

Throughout high school you should keep a list of all your involvements outside of school. I guarantee that the fund-raising walk you did in tenth grade will slip your mind two years later when you sit down to write your extracurricular list. By keeping a running list, you will be sure not to leave out important commitments and events that took up a significant amount of time. Learn to be a good record keeper.

list your
involvements

< 42 >

> Excellence is evident

Take the high road when reporting your
extracurricular activities on a college application.
Paint a clear picture of how you spent your free
time, and make sure you don't sell yourself
short. You don't have to go overboard, however,
to prove your involvement. The outline and
description of activities will illuminate your
excellence.

Take the high road

< 43 >

Three

Summer Plans

> Get Beyond the Beach Vacation

A journey of a thousand miles begins with but a single step.

—Chinese proverb

> Don't wait until the summer before applying to college to get involved in academic activities

High school freshmen, sophomores, and juniors should make good use of their summers. Many of the top summer programs at colleges and private schools fill up well ahead of the spring deadlines, so plan ahead. Focus on your academic interests: if you like science, make sure you check out top science-oriented programs. Remember, sometimes financial aid is available on a need basis, so don't be shy about applying. The Internet is a good first step to sifting out your options. Check strong programs like Cornell's summer school, Columbia's, Andover's, and many others. Advance planning now will come in handy later when you find yourself scrambling to finish these applications by the appropriate deadlines. For now, at least request information from five to ten programs. (See Resources on pages 221–229)

< 46 >

> An Opportunity to Have Fun and Discover Yourself

Sometimes it's important to work for that pot of gold. But other times it's essential to take time off and to make sure that your most important decision in the day simply consists of choosing which color to slide down on the rainbow.
—Douglas Pagels, author

> Start early

No matter what it is you are planning, summer opportunities or starting your college essays, begin early. We feel the most anxiety when we are up against a time wall and therefore aren't as effective in our choices. So start designing your perfect summer right around Thanksgiving. Call for catalogs, use online search engines, talk to local vendors who may need summer employ- ment help. By beginning early, you can craft a thoughtful, well-rounded summer that nurtures your body, mind, and spirit. And you won't hear "sorry we've already filled that position."

< 47 >

> Get a Job

Many students think that doing community service will get them into top colleges, but that's no longer the case. The truth is that many high schools require community service, so it's difficult to tell who put their heart into it and who did it because it was required. If you want a more productive use of your time both during the year and during the summer, get a job! Or if you're too young to work a real job, start your own business (see page 38)—dog walking, house-sitting, whatever! Not only does holding down a job show responsibility, it also shows that you're not a spoiled, pampered child who has never had to work. Remember, most admissions officers reading your file probably held a job at your age. Don't delay!

Be productive

> Let go

Try not to get upset over those things you can't do anything about. If a problem is beyond your control, try your best to accept it until it can be changed. So you don't have the funds to attend the science camp you've been nominated for—rather than seeing this as a problem, see it as an opportunity to use your creativity. Ask about financial aid, or approach a local community group that might consider sponsoring you. Or look at it as divine order or fate, and begin another quest for a way to combine your love of science with making some money. How about a job in your local hospital's lab?

Accept what can't be changed

< 49 >

> Mix in some academic programs

Not all your summer work needs to have an academic focus, but try to maintain a balance. It's reasonable to spend two to four weeks each summer doing something intellectual in a field that interests you, which still gives you many weeks for visiting colleges, hanging out with friends, working, or vacationing with your family.

maintain a balance

< 50 >

> Take time to unwind

When planning your summer, make sure to create "stress release time." No schedule. No agenda. Pick a relaxing place and a simple agenda. The ultimate goal is to "detox" from the pressures of daily life. In fact, why wait for the summer? Put a "chill out weekend" or "down-shift evening" on your calendar.

No schedule
No agenda

< 51 >

> It's okay to vacation with your family

Keep in mind that colleges look at trends. If you have done research every summer for five straight summers, admissions officers will see your love of research. That doesn't mean you can't save a few weeks of the summer for family time. If you do academic work all summer after a brutal academic year, you will simply burn out.

family time

< 52 >

> Foster and deepen your close relationships

Don't craft a summer that is so busy that you don't have time to spend with the people you love. All too soon you will most likely be living apart from your family and childhood friends, so reach out and make even closer connections this summer. It might mean taking the initiative to organize a family weekend activity or launching a business with two pals who have similar interests.

Make connections

< 53 >

> Don't do it just to get into college

This point is important both for your own sanity and for college purposes. College admissions officers are sharp—it will be obvious if you did your only academic program the summer before applying to college. In short, don't do something simply because it "looks good." What really looks good to admissions officers is when students follow their own interests and pursue them in novel and interesting ways.

follow your own interests

< 54 >

> No one says you HAVE to . . .

Stress kicks in when you are inauthentic—when you try to be someone you aren't. Doing something you don't love can drag you down in all areas of your life. There's enough of that during the school year. Craft a summer that is a wonderful balance of enrichment, service, and fun.

Have fun

< 55 >

> Use summers to schedule early campus visits

Don't wait until junior year! Try to fit in campus visits around family vacations or add some weekend trips to campuses near you. That way you'll have some idea of what type of campus you like.

Take a weekend trip

< 56 >

> Grab the opportunity to try something new

Summer is ideal for trying something completely
different. If you've always wanted to rock climb,
use a part of this summer to follow your desire.
Life can become much too regimented as you
move out of high school, so embrace something
new now. Learn how to knit, speak Chinese, perform mime, or play the drums. Don't be afraid
that you won't succeed; summer is your opportunity to take a risk and have fun in the process.
You can always write a college application essay
about the experience.

try something new

< 57 >

> Be sure to keep a record of what you do every summer

When you write your activity sheet for every college, there is always a separate section (or you can make one) for summer activities. You'll want to list all the academic programs you've attended, any jobs, and anyone you've worked for who may write you a recommendation letter.

summer activities

< 58 >

> Make the most of whatever summer plans you do decide upon

If you've managed to land a job, get to know your supervisor and find out how you can be the most help. No, you don't want to flip burgers for the rest of your life, but entering into the scene fully, engaging those around you, and offering everything you can only enhances the experience. You can also ask for recommendations at the end of the gig, as well as a job for next summer if you so desire.

enhance the experience

> Be sure to fill up your summers with the reading you don't have time to do during the year

Now that the SAT has changed to reflect more reading comprehension, it is imperative to train your mind to focus for one to two hours at a time to read challenging material. Summer is the time to read all of Jane Austen or five Charles Dickens novels. During the school year you may be stuck with required reading, but during the summers you can focus on the longer novels that will make you a better reader.

read

< 60 >

> Soulful reading can change your life

There are some amazing books available at any library that can inspire, support, and guide you. Use the summer months to explore an area of literature that you might not feel you have time for during the year. Herman Hesse's classic *Siddhartha* is the story of Prince Siddhartha's path to enlightenment and is just one example of books about spiritual models who have gone before us.

explore literature

< 61 >

> Collect words

From eighth grade onward you should buy a spiral notebook and keep vocabulary words in it. The new SAT reflects knowledge of vocabulary in context, so the sooner you start, the sooner you will acquire a large reading vocabulary. Rather than just writing definitions, be sure to write the word in the context you found it. For example, if the word is sycophantic, you should write down, "His sycophantic behavior made his classmates hate him."

Broaden your vocabulary

< 62 >

> Collect memories

For most of you the summer will be a downshift in your frantic school year pace. Use this slower rhythm to spend time with your family. Your time living under the same roof year-round is drawing to an end. You want to enjoy time with your family, as it adds to the texture of who you are. Yes, qualitative aspects of your personality are important for college admissions. Loving your family makes you a happier person. Happier people make better college students . . . see where I am going with this?

enjoy time with your family

< 63 >

> Wrap it up

Finally, use the summer before you senior year to finish as many applications as you can. Even though they are not due until November 1 for early decision (January 1 for regular decision), colleges scrutinize senior fall grades to assure themselves that your grade trend is heading upward. Since you will no doubt have a difficult course load, you want to spend senior fall concentrating on your courses and trying to get all A's, not scrambling at the last minute to finish your college applications!

Avoid last-minute scrambling

< 64 >

> Organize in a relaxed mode

When you aren't rushed, you can actually enjoy the college admissions process. The August before your senior year is a good time to kick back and play with your essay ideas as well as organize your list of college data. A spreadsheet with college name, application deadline, essay requirements, and other important information is a great tool for staying organized and on top of deadlines.

Relax and enjoy

< 65 >

Four

Standardized Testing

> It Does Matter

*Stress is when you wake up screaming, and
then realize that you haven't fallen asleep yet.*
                                    —Unknown

> Don't wait until junior or senior year

Since most students will need to take the SAT I
several times and then three SAT II subject tests,
plus Advanced Placement (AP) or International
Baccalaureate (IB) tests, it is a much better idea to
get some of the testing done early. If you're good
at math, take the Math IIC your sophomore year.
If you're fluent in Spanish, take the Spanish SAT II
early on. Don't ever take three SAT II subject tests
on the same date; you will almost certainly score
lower on all three of the tests than you would if
you took only one or two per sitting.

< 68 >

> Tap In to Your Laser Thinking

Nothing contributes so much to tranquilizing the mind as a steady purpose—a point on which the soul may fix its intellectual eye.
                —Mary Wollstonecraft Shelley

> Identify what, if anything, about standardized testing causes you anxiety

Knowledge is power, and just knowing that you find the timing element, for instance, daunting can help you work on techniques to conquer that fear. Not only will this awareness help with your standardized tests, but it can also help with your regular school exams. In fact, knowing what makes you feel the most anxious is knowledge that will help you manage stress all of your life.

< 69 >

> Learn the ins and outs of each SAT II

Some tests have much higher average scores than others! For example, many more students score in the 700s on the Math IIC than on the Math IC. The Chinese SAT II test has an average close to a perfect score! Do your research, and figure out which tests are the best match for your interests and which ones throw you out of the 700 range when you miss only a few questions. You'll do better on the biology SAT II if you wait until after you've taken AP Biology (as many students do, hence the curve), but American history can be taken without the AP, which has a different focus. Study the tests, and take the ones that best showcase your abilities.

study the tests

< 70 >

> Use your laser thinking

You *do* have laser thinking, and test taking is just the time to tap in to this way of focusing. Think of the power of a flashlight beam cutting through the darkness, lighting up everything in its path. This is what your laser thinking can do. You can cut through the fog and illuminate each question. Focus directly and completely on the task in front of you—the test. Hone your mind as if you're directing a powerful laser, slicing through any matter. Cut through the distractions in the room or voices of doubt in your head. You might go so far as to imagine you are wearing a funky pair of blinders similar to what horses wear in horse races. Know that you can tap in to the power of your focused mind at any time.

FOCUS

< 71 >

> Figure out which test is best for you

In certain cases, it may be more beneficial for you to take the SAT instead of the ACT, or vice versa. Be careful, though, because college officials are suspicious if someone from an East Coast city like New York starts taking the ACT because they think they'll do better. For the most part, the ACT is used by Midwestern schools, so study for it and take it only if you come from an area where many students actually sit for the ACT. Colleges don't like scheming students.

Take the best for you

< 72 >

> Make test-taking time as relaxing as possible

Dress in your most comfortable clothes for the test. Pajamas and your favorite bunny slippers are just fine if that's how you are most at ease. Create a "comfort" kit for your test day. Pack a pillow to place behind your back, a thermos of your favorite "stress buster" tea, and even your CD player with soothing music to pop on during the breaks.

Be comfortable

< 73 >

> Plan carefully to avoid too many test sittings

Now that the College Board has eliminated score choice, you have to send all of your test scores to colleges. This means that colleges can see how many times you've taken every test. If a college sees that you've taken the SAT five times, they may start to think you could be doing something more productive with your time than taking the SAT over and over again.

Plan carefully

< 74 >

> Practice moderation

This isn't a race to take as many tests as you can pack into your last two years of high school. Don't let testing rule your life. Use your discernment and know when enough is enough. Think of all the good you could be doing in your community or in your family rather than sitting for endless numbers of tests.

Don't let testing rule your life

< 75 >

> Do your SAT prep before the junior year PSAT

Colleges buy lists of high PSAT scorers, so doing well on the PSAT will put you on the mailing list of hundreds of top colleges. In addition, each state has a different formula for determining National Merit status, but all of them use the junior year PSAT to compute who will become a National Merit Finalist.

Do your SAT prep early

< 76 >

> Set up a study schedule

It's a good idea to set up a specific schedule during the year to help you study for any upcoming standardized test. For instance, Wednesday evenings from 9:00 to 10:00 PM during your sophomore year might be the time you designate for going over the PSAT study guides you have purchased. Sunday morning may be when you add two new words to your vocabulary list. The idea is that you have created this date with yourself to build your skills over time. That way, you won't have the inevitable stress that comes with cramming when the test is days away.

Don't cram

< 77 >

> Don't sign up for AP classes unless you plan on taking the AP exams

Colleges will assume you are shying away from a challenge if you take an AP class but then don't bother to sit for the exam. You want to portray yourself as the kind of student who loves challenges, not the kind who runs away. The AP exams are rigorous tests, and colleges actually weigh them more than SAT I's and II's since they compare favorably to college work. Becoming an AP scholar with honors or distinction is a very high level award that impresses even the most competitive colleges. If your school has the International Baccalaureate program (IB), go for the full diploma, not just a few discrete courses. Not many students reach a high enough level to achieve the full IB diploma (the collection of courses and community service requirements set out by the administrators of the IB organization in Geneva), so make yourself stand out.

take the AP exams

< 78 >

> ## Creative visualization is one of the most powerful techniques for living the life of your dreams

Visualizing doesn't mean you don't take action; sorry, you can't skip the SATs. It does mean you can use the power of your imagination to visualize what you want to unfold in your life. In fact, you are probably using this tool now and you don't even realize it. All you have to do is relax and picture in your mind the details of what you want to manifest. So picture yourself calmly taking the standardized tests, knowing the correct answers and feeling confident. Visualize yourself calm and at peace as you open the letter revealing stellar results on your standardized tests. Feel the feelings of doing the best job possible.

use the power of your imagination

> Don't wait weeks for your scores

Did you know that once you take the SAT I's or II's, you no longer have to wait months for your test to be scored? If you do nothing, you won't receive your scores for several weeks, but if you look on the College Board Web site, you'll note that you can pay a small fee and get your scores by phone around ten days after the test. As a student, it's beneficial to find out early so you can decide whether you want to include those scores on any early applications you may be sending in. It will also give you a better idea of which colleges are good potential matches. When you sit for a test, always find out the exact day that you can call to find out your scores.

find out early

< 80 >

> Sleep, sleep, and sleep some more the day before your test

Research shows that extra cramming is counter-productive the day before a test or exam, but an extra hour or two of sleep will keep you sharp and on top of your game. Don't even consider sleeping pills, however, as you will only feel groggy the day of the test. Drop some lavender oil on your pillow, and clear your bedroom of anything having to do with the test, creating an oasis of calm and peace.

Get some sleep

< 81 >

> On the Math SAT I, remember that the most difficult questions are at the end of each section

If they seem too easy, you are probably not getting the right answer. If you're not aiming for a perfect 800, feel free to leave the last few questions in each math section blank so you can dedicate time to getting as many correct as you can.

Leave them blank

< 82 >

> Read and your scores go up

Studies show that kids who are voracious readers have much higher SAT scores. So make it a habit to unwind each evening by reading before sleep. Turn off the computer, dim the lights, and crack open that latest piece of fiction. It's a great way to transition from your hectic day to dreamland while upping your verbal score.

Be a voracious reader

< 83 >

> Reading comprehension strategy

If you're a slow reader, pick the most difficult reading comprehension passage and leave it blank. Spend your time getting as many questions right as you can on the passages you can read slowly and carefully. The test rewards correct answers and does not "punish" for wrong answers. You can always go back and tackle the passage you skipped if you finish the other passages with time to spare.

You can always go back

< 84 >

> In an emergency, call a halt

If you get a bloody nose in the middle of your test, for instance, and spend more time trying to stop the bleeding than focusing on the questions, call the test monitor over and have him or her document your problem. Finish the test, but know that you have twenty-four hours to decide if you want to cancel the scores. Don't worry, emergencies happen, and the College Board has a system for putting a halt to your scores in these circumstances.

emergencies happen

< 85 >

> Be careful if you skip a question

Take an extra second or two every time you answer a question to make sure your answer sheet matches your test booklet. In other words, if you skip a question, double-check that you are skipping the question on your answer sheet too. One missed space can mean hundreds of points on the actual test if all of your answers are out of place. Also, when you leave blank a question you might be able to figure out with additional time, put a star by it so you can come back quickly to it if you have some extra time.

Be careful

< 86 >

> Don't doubt yourself

Be careful not to overthink each question. Often the first answer you come up with is right, but that nasty self-doubt can sway you from your instincts. Trust yourself here and move on to the next question.

Trust yourself

< 87 >

Five

Narrow the
Search

> Pick the School That's Right for You

Just remember, 100% of the shots you don't take, don't go in.

—Wayne Gretzky

> Investigate special programs

What is the college you're looking at known for? Strong engineering programs, study abroad programs, research opportunities? Take the time to ask what programs make the school stand out, and think seriously about whether you'd be a good match for those programs. Conversely, if you love foreign languages and there is no study-abroad program, look elsewhere for programs that suit your needs.

< 90 >

> The Right Place at the Right Time

The Creator gives us each a song.

—Ute saying

> Remain open to surprises

Rather than assuming that the list of colleges you create is final and unalterable, lighten up and realize this is a fluid, organic process. Try saying these words: "My decisions are made by following my deepest intuition. I let go of fear. I trust that everything is in perfect order. I do the footwork but keep myself open to ideas, insight, and information that adds to my quest." Or write the following on an index card and post it where you will see it every day: "I draw to me and I accept the college that is right for me. The process is enjoyable and calm."

< 91 >

> Pay attention to admissions statistics

Many students I work with start out with unrealistic expectations. If the average SAT scores at a college are 1400 and you have a 1250, chances are you will not be admitted unless there are some outstanding characteristics that would make you stand out. If 94 percent of the admitted class comes from the top 10 percent of their high school class and you are only in the top 30 percent, odds are you will not be accepted.

Pay attention

< 92 >

> It's about the "fit" for you, not the label

Remind yourself that college is not simply another "thing" you purchase with a definitive outline of what is and isn't the "best." Education is not a commodity, as much as the ranking services will tell you otherwise, but rather an opportunity to gain understanding and wisdom. Approached from this perspective, you can narrow the colleges you add to your list with an eye toward "how might this place deepen my deeper understanding of myself, my interests, and what I can ultimately give to the world." College is only a part of your journey toward more wisdom.

It's about the "fit"

< 93 >

> Use early programs to your advantage

Despite what colleges want you to believe, getting in early usually gives you a much higher admit rate. For the class of 2004 at Yale for example, the early admit rate was 37 percent versus only 16 percent for the regular rate. Do your research, and try to apply to one or more colleges using early action, early decision, and early rolling policies to your advantage. The difference can be dramatic.

Do your research

< 94 >

> Infuse your college search process with questions about a school's moral and spiritual climate

How does the institution address academic honesty, service, leadership, substance abuse prevention, faith communities, and emotional support? Are there religious groups that you wish to join? Is there a sense of inclusion on campus or strongly divided belief systems? All of this information can paint a picture of a place that will nourish your spirit or leave you feeling cold.

Ask questions

< 95 >

> Rural versus urban

Are you a city person? Are you comfortable in a very rural and isolated environment? Do you prefer a Starbucks on every corner? The first big distinction you'll want to make in your college search is between rural and urban campuses. You'll want to explain to each college why you are applying, but if you feel no deep convictions about the campus or have serious reservations, you should not even bother to apply.

Make the distinction

< 96 >

> Get in touch with where you feel the most comfortable

Does spending time in the city give you joy? Or are you happiest when hiking long, wooded trails? A college exists that perfectly suits all of your needs. The important thing is to know yourself well and articulate what kind of school nurtures that self. This is four years of your life, so you want there to be good "college shui," along with good *feng shui*, of course.

good "college shui"

< 97 >

> Liberal arts versus research institutions

Are you a science whiz who needs top-notch facilities, or a poetry freak who would love to sit out in a pasture and think about nature? Do you want small, intimate classes, or can you learn equally well in large lecture courses? The second biggest feature to consider is whether you'd like to attend a liberal arts college or a major research institution. Neither one is more prestigious inherently—the choice is personal and very much related to your own academic interests. Be sure to look at specific departments within the schools you are applying to so you can make sure they meet your needs. If you want to study Sanskrit, you'll want to choose a school with a strong ancient languages department.

Personal choice

< 98 >

> Be realistic, but don't give up your dreams

I'm a firm advocate for going for our dreams, but
we must also sprinkle common sense and logic
into the equation. If you have always dreamed of
attending Harvard, for instance, but you are a C
student in the fall of your senior year, then let's
tweak the dream. Harvard runs an extension
school with classes that meet in the evenings.
Harvard professors teach these rich, top-level
classes that are open to anyone. Perhaps you
could attend Harvard, but via another route. So
dig deep into the essence of your dreams and then
manage your expectations and take appropriate
action. There is no sense in stressing out for a
dream that clearly needs to be altered.

*manage your
expectations*

< 99 >

> Let your teachers know your plans

You'll want to ask recent teachers (eleventh and twelfth grade, not ninth and tenth in most cases) to write recommendations for you well ahead of time. Once you have a "short" list (or even before you do), approach two teachers whom you believe would have the most to say about your academic performance, and ask if they'd feel comfortable writing one of your principal college recommendations for you. If they hesitate, ask someone else who is more gung ho. They should be pleased, not put out, if you've been a real contributor. Don't worry if the teacher is a brilliant writer or not—colleges look for the content, so all it takes is a few sentences to say you're the best student in the past twenty years!

ask recent teachers

< 100 >

> Show your appreciation

Many students simply *expect* their teachers to write letters for them, but remember that recommendations are time-consuming for your teachers and a critical part of the college admissions picture for you. Identify the appropriate teachers, ask if they'd mind writing on your behalf, and then if they say yes, provide them with stamped, addressed envelopes so all they have to do is write the letter and fill in the appropriate check boxes. They shouldn't have to do anything extra like fill in your name and Social Security number on the official sheets or look for postage. Sometime after they have written the letter (around Thanksgiving or Christmas is a good time), buy them a thoughtful present and write a note expressing your thanks.

express your thanks

< 101 >

> Contact professors

If you are interested in a very specialized area, say particle physics, use the Internet and e-mail to contact a specific professor at a school you're interested in, and share your research interests. That way they can fill you in on how strong that program is and what other programs are worth considering. Professors are the best source of the real inside scoop on which departments are the best. One of my students asked a professor during her visit which school has the best art history program, and without hesitation, the professor mentioned a competitor school as having by far the top program. You can't get that kind of information in a guide.

Professors are the best source

< 102 >

> E-mail can lessen contact anxiety

The beauty of sending an e-mail rather than making a phone call is that you can thoughtfully compose your missive to a professor, department head, coach, or director. E-mail doesn't require you to think on your feet, as does a phone call, or require the cumbersome response that letters call for, like a return letter or phone call. E-mail doesn't interrupt someone and can be a polite initial contact. Take your time in crafting any e-mail you send to college personnel. Make sure you begin with a well-researched reason for contacting the person in the first place. "I have read your book on quantum physics as well as the article you presented in Journal X. It is my dream to study in your department at College Y and . . ."

Send an e-mail
instead

< 103 >

> Use your contacts

Once you've initiated contacts with professors, use these contacts to your advantage. Often professors who have gotten to know students by speaking to them or reviewing their research will write strong letters of recommendation to the admissions office. If a professor says he'd love to have you in his program, college admissions offices take note!

use your contacts

< 104 >

> Don't apply to a school just because your boyfriend or girlfriend goes there

I'm all for following your heart, except when it leads you to a college just because you are in love—not with the school but with someone who attends. What's right for your boyfriend or girlfriend may not be a good fit for you. If the two of you were meant to be together, your choice of school won't keep you apart.

Love the school

< 105 >

> Do your homework

Many colleges are abolishing fraternities. Would you prefer a college with fraternities and sororities or one that has a different social feel? Middlebury College in Vermont decided to take the gorgeous houses that were for fraternities and convert them to high-quality campus housing. Many students believe the campus is less intimidating and more social now that the fraternities are gone. Ask each college what they do to promote healthy or alternative lifestyles.

fraternities

< 106 >

> Tune in to the social tone

Figure out what kind of social atmosphere you would like in a college. Some schools have great school spirit and almost all students attend sporting events, for instance, whereas other colleges are empty on the weekends. Do you want fraternities and sororities? Are you looking for an ethnically diverse place? Just articulating the kind of culture that you are looking for is half the battle of finding the perfect school match.

social atmosphere

< 107 >

> Use the Internet

The Internet is a great tool. Many Web sites let
you enter your major interests, hobbies, and
passions and then create a list of colleges. Even
the yearly *U.S. News and World Report Rankings*
will let you enter demographic information so
that you can narrow your college choice and sort
through thousands of colleges.

the Internet

< 108 >

> Create your perfect school scenario

Daydream a little and picture your ideal college profile. What size is the school, is it co-ed or single sex, what's the setting, who are the professors, what is the social tone, the cost? Finding the right college fit will be a lot easier when you take the time to do this exercise. You might even create a collage of pictures and words describing the essence of what you are looking for in a college. Call it your "College Treasure Map" and post it on your bedroom wall for inspiration.

Daydream a little

< 109 >

Six

Application Strategies

> The Nitty Gritty

*You've got to think about "big things" while
you're doing small things, so that all the small
things go in the right direction.*

—Alvin Toffler

> Make it personal

Many students make the mistake of writing
about other people, like a grandparent, a teacher,
or an influential mentor. The problem is, the college learns only about that other person and not
enough about you! So write about yourself, your
interest areas, your hobbies, your academic aspi-
rations, not about other people.

< 112 >

> Enjoy the Process

We forfeit three-fourths of ourselves to be like other people.

—Arthur Schopenhauer

> Scan the list of essay questions on every application

Which essay question gives you a "zing?" Don't be swayed by the one you think will make you appear a certain way, well traveled, smart, savvy. Instead, follow your passion and write about the topic that speaks to you. Believe in your voice. Trust yourself to translate your thoughts, experiences, and unique self to the page!

< 113 >

> Take the time to say *why*

Given two similar applicants, colleges will always
select the one who shows the most interest in his
or her school. Why? The answer is simple—yield.
Colleges care a lot about numbers and the yield,
or how many students accept their offer of
admission, an important statistic for them. So
take the time to write a specific paragraph about
what particular programs interest you and why
you would be a good match for the school.

say why

> Don't hide your true feelings

If you love a college, let the admissions department know. Fire off an e-mail letting the person
who interviewed you know that after completing
all of your college tours your heart is set on his
or her college or university. Don't be inauthentic,
but rather be honest and enthusiastic about why
the school resonated so perfectly with your
hopes, dreams, and wishes. This is no time to
play hard-to-get. Being honest is a lot less
stressful than pretending.

Be honest

> Don't leave out your AP or IB scores

One fault of the common application is that there is not a separate space for AP or IB scores. Just use the empty white space to the right of your other SAT I and SAT II scores to write in your AP/IB scores, even though there is not an "official" space for them.

use the empty space

< 116 >

> Map out your high school courses early on

In order to have your AP and IB classes count for admissions purposes, they must be taken by your junior year. Rather than putting off all your AP classes until your senior year, try to fit some in during tenth and eleventh grade so you can present colleges with some strong AP/IB scores.

Map it out

< 117 >

> Have a trusted friend read your materials

You don't want to edit your voice out of the essay, so for the most part, your parents are not the best people to look over the application for you. However, friends can usually do a decent job eliminating major typos and make helpful suggestions about how to let your voice shine through.

Let your voice shine through

< 118 >

> Who are you?

How are you "doing life?" Take a deep breath
here. Can you paint a picture of yourself as if
looking down on your life from above? Free
write for ten minutes describing this person.
Now, make sure the essence of who you are is
translated to the application in some way.

*paint a picture of
yourself*

< 119 >

> Don't feel limited by the application

Even though the common application (and many college applications) only ask for a short "most meaningful activity" essay and a general main essay, feel free to include one or two extra essays that explain your other interests, hobbies, or passions. Don't let the application limit what you have to say—simply include extra information with your name and Social Security number (in case it gets lost) and title it "Extra Essay."

Write an extra essay

< 120 >

> Connect with your inner self

If you find yourself worried about a particular
aspect of the application, ask your inner
guidance if there is some action you might take
to move closer to a resolution. You might ask this
before falling asleep at night, then pay attention
to your dreams, your first thoughts in the
morning, or simply wait for an answer to appear.
Througout the next day keep a notebook to jot
down ideas as they float into your mind.

ask your inner
guide

< 121 >

> Take the time to explain any anomalies, even if they don't ask

Most applications don't have a separate question that allows you to explain any extenuating circumstances, but often students would be well served to write a short note. If someone in your family had a major health problem in your tenth grade year that necessitated your spending time caring for them (and your grades suffered as a result), by all means write a brief note. Don't make excuses, but do fill in the details of why your grades dropped. If the event didn't affect your performance, there's no need to include it.

explain extenuating circumstances

< 122 >

> Be honest

Even if you have been sanctioned by your school for some action, it's better that you bring it up and explain the problem. The last thing you want is someone else to mention an ethical problem that you have omitted. Oftentimes there are innocent explanations for suspensions—college admissions officers were kids, too, and will often laugh at pranks that may have warranted disciplinary action from the school. There's a big difference between being suspended for organizing a rally against a new policy and for coming to school drunk—explain yourself and be up front. Not being fully honest takes a lot more energy and causes much more stress than owning up to the truth—both on your college applications and in life.

explain the problem

> Don't feel you have to type your application

Many students stress out over having to type their applications. For the major essays you can use the computer and word-process them, but for the short biographical part one sections, just use a pen and handwrite the information. Colleges even prefer handwritten responses to short questions, since it tells them you didn't just send your application to your parents' office to have someone else do it for you (which is what admissions officers will assume). You are a student, and it's okay to look like one; in fact, it's more authentic if you take the time to handwrite this section. On a similar note, it's fine for you to white out or cross out a word. You don't want to make a mess, but you do want to make it look personal.

make it look personal

< 124 >

> Sometimes anxiety can be a good thing

Natural anxiety will help you remain alert to the action you need to take to complete your applications. When you feel a surge of anxiety, get busy identifying the steps you must act on to move to completion. Write them down. Then, next to the steps you must take, create a timeline for completing them.

use your anxiety

> Don't use the common application as a crutch

Though some colleges like Harvard use the common application exactly as their own, it's better to use the school's own application forms unless you fall into a lower socio-economic background. Don't be lazy—even if you use the common application, don't just photocopy it. Write out a few hand-prepared copies. The main part is only four pages of mostly biographical information, and the major essays should all be typed anyway.

Write it out

< 126 >

> Reward yourself

Make a pact with a friend to go out for dinner
when you both finish your applications. Set a
specific deadline and reserve a table at your
favorite restaurant so that you remain committed
to that date. If you feel more rewarded with
other lures, plan that reward. Maybe you decide
to buy yourself the biking shoes you've wanted,
but only after completing all your essays. You get
the picture.

Reward yourself

< 127 >

> Personalize your application

For the computer-processed short essays, at least put the name of each school on top to personalize them. That way you at least convey you are thinking about that particular school, not just applying to a random selection of colleges. The common application has taken a lot of the personality out of each application, so be sure to print out slightly different versions of your essays for each school. It only takes a few extra moments to make each application look like it was prepared for that particular school.

Make it personal

< 128 >

> Make it festive

Filling out applications can become a fun
process rather than dreary drudgework when
you embrace it with a celebratory attitude. Purchase a special application pen and funky folders
for all the forms. Burn an "application CD" of
music that inspires you. Light a candle when you
begin application work to mark the time as a
special event.

*Applications can
be fun*

> Be mindful of deadlines and special rules

Some colleges, like the University of Michigan, have rolling early programs, so the earlier you mail in your application (as in September), the earlier you will receive a response and the better your chance of admission will be. Others, like Harvard and Yale, have strict rules: they are "single action, early action," which means if you plan to apply there, you cannot apply to other schools under their early programs. Stay within ethical boundaries and respect the colleges' rules.

Be mindful

< 130 >

> Put it away

After filling out your application, get some distance. Put it away for a day or two, then go back
and read the application with a discerning eye.
Act as if you are the admissions officer reading
this application for the first time. Be very critical
and read with an editor's eye.

get some distance

< 131 >

Seven

Write a Winning Essay

> How to Separate the "Men from the Boys"

The thing always happens that you really believe in; and the belief in a thing makes it happen.

—Frank Lloyd Wright

> Don't try to recount your whole life in one essay

The best essays take a small "slice" of life and expand that into an essay. You may want to choose a specific moment or incident in your life that changed the way you think or the way you operate and explain the mental change that took place.

> Your Words Have Power

Experience is not what happens to you; it is what you do with what happens to you.
—Aldous Huxley, author, philosopher

> Write the essay

DON'T EVEN THINK OF HIRING SOMEONE TO WRITE YOUR ESSAY FOR YOU. Your essay is an opportunity to express yourself, not to become unethical. Elizabeth Dole told the Duke University class of 2000, "In the final analysis, it is your moral compass that counts far more than any bank balance, any resume, and yes, any diploma."

< 135 >

> Don't put the reader to sleep

If your essay is boring to you, it will be boring to others as well. Ask yourself (or ask a friend) if the essence of who you are comes across—don't be packaged, be yourself.

be yourself

< 136 >

> Brainstorming taps your inner genius

Make sure you allow time for free-flow writing.
Grab a blank piece of paper and simply begin
filling it without lifting your pen. (Somehow
brainstorming with a pen and paper taps in to
your creativity more than typing on the computer.) Bring the essay question to mind, then
begin writing. Don't worry about grammar, sen-
tence structure, or even staying on topic. This
is the greasing of the wheel that will allow you
to then narrow the ideas you've created.

grease the wheel

< 137 >

> Don't be afraid to be funny, but don't write a joke essay

You can let your humor shine through, but don't devote your whole essay to a humorous topic. College admissions offices are looking for students with strong intellects, not comedians, although of course occasional humor is okay.

let your humor shine

< 138 >

> If you are stumped, begin with the title

Often your creative channels can be opened if you approach an essay by playing with titles. A funny, clever, or mysterious title can be just the spark you need to fly into the essay itself.

begin with the title

< 139 >

> Spell-check and edit

You'd be surprised how many students forget to run a spell check. While a typo here and there won't kill your chances, it is careless to let your work be sloppy and unprofessional. As with your applications, have a friend or teacher read your essays for errors. Be sure when you've personalized parts of your essay to change the name of the school.

Look for errors

< 140 >

> Picture your way to essay bliss

A photograph or another visual prompt can be
the impetus you need to craft a compelling essay.
If you are writing about a past experience, find a
photo of that event. Place the photo in front of
you to bring back the sensations of the day—the
color of the sky, smells, what you wore. If you
don't have a photograph, find one that elicits
similar feelings. Go through magazines and tear
out pictures that might have the essence of your
essay topic. If you love the French language and
culture, a van Gogh painting may inspire you to
illustrate in words your quest to become fluent,
for instance.

use a photo

< 141 >

> Avoid clichéd topics

If you want a list of the most abused essay topics, buy and read a very funny book called *Writing the College Essay* by Harry Bauld. Not only will you laugh out loud, but you'll also learn which topics (your stuffed animal, your room decor) are death to the applicant in terms of impressing admissions officers.

Avoid clichéd topics

< 142 >

> Set realistic standards and deadlines

Don't think you can wait until the last minute to write a winning essay. Ideas take time to stew and ferment. Build in time so you can dump essay ideas onto the page, then sit with them for a while before polishing and editing. Be realistic and set workable goals. Start simply, maybe by brainstorming five great lead sentences to choose from.

Ideas take time

< 143 >

> Don't overpackage or edit out your own voice

This is why you should not show your essays to your parents. You don't want to sound like an adult writing the essay, you want to sound like an actual kid applying to college. I'm not saying you should be sloppy, but rather that you should let your voice shine through.

Don't overpackage

< 144 >

> Read your writing aloud

After you've completed your essay draft, read it to yourself aloud. You'll find out what works and doesn't work from hearing your piece. You'll also "hear" where to add depth or a punctuation mark. So close your door, forget your inhibitions, and listen to your essay.

Read it aloud

< 145 >

> Be unconventional

Remember that admissions officers read for eight
to ten hours a day during high season, so you
can only imagine how one applicant blends into
another. Therefore, if you have interesting or
thought-provoking views, write about them. Too
many students aim to please when they should
be aiming to stimulate conversation or to convey
how they think and process information.

Be unconventional

< 146 >

> Tell the truth

Be willing to write deeply and honestly. When you go into the truthful places of your life, the most dimensional essays seem to appear. So if you were scared senseless the first time you ran a class meeting, write about that feeling—honestly—without being ashamed. Tell how your hands shook and you couldn't catch your breath. Flash back in time, get inside your body and describe it. Then, when you fast-forward to running your fifteenth meeting with assurance, the contrast will be vivid.

write deeply and honestly

< 147 >

> Write the big essays first

Write what you want to write about and then go back and come up with the question to fit your essay later. Many college applications let you write your own question (even the common application has that option) for your main essay, so write what you want to write about and make up the question last rather than trying to fit your entire being into the confines of a restricting essay question.

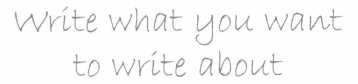

Write what you want to write about

< 148 >

> Get active

Scan your essay again and again to strike any words that take it out of the active voice. I know—you learned this in eighth grade! But we can all use a reminder. Avoid words such as: is, am, could, might, shall, were, was, and should.

Get active

< 149 >

> To thine own self be true

Don't misrepresent yourself to colleges. Many
students are tempted to exaggerate or lie about
their accomplishments, but in my experience,
this almost always backfires. It's better to show
colleges what you are really like rather than what
you think they want you to be. Honesty is the
best policy.

Don't exaggerate

< 150 >

> Get real

Ask your friends and family what stands out about you, and use that as a focus for your essay topic. Don't attempt to write what you "think" college admissions officers want to read, but rather spend time writing about your unique place in this world.

what stands out
about you

< 151 >

> Don't forget to personalize your essays

Even though undoubtedly you will end up using one or more essays for several schools, take the time to make each one look as if it were prepared for that school by putting a heading with the school name. There is nothing worse than ending your Harvard essay with, "and this is why I want to attend Yale." Do take the time to explain why you are applying to each school, even if the application doesn't specifically ask that question.

Get personal

> You don't need to shout

The essay doesn't have to be a "shout out" of your greatest accomplishments. Sometimes the most mundane aspect of your life can pack the most powerful punch. Drop down into your deepest intuitive place and look for ideas and inspiration. What experience in your life was truly meaningful to you? Don't worry how it will "read," just trust. If you do write about something you've accomplished, don't fret about appearing to brag. Lots of kids are afraid their essay will appear to be a banner ad about themselves. There's a fine balance. You'll know the difference.

Find the balance

< 153 >

Eight

Campus Visits

> It's a Wide World Out There

Happiness, wealth, and success are the by-products of goal-setting; they cannot be the goal themselves.

—John Condry

> Envision yourself on the campus

During your visit to campus, check out the dorm rooms, the dining hall, the library, the classrooms, and visualize what it would be like to be a student. If you don't feel comfortable or you can't see yourself studying in the library, chances are the school is not for you. Are the students you meet friendly? Inviting? Would you want to spend four years with them? Ask yourself these questions as you walk around the campus.

> Scan for Qualities That You Hold Dear

Clear intuition requires the ability to respect your own impressions.

—Caroline Myss, author

> Call early

Can I say it again? Planning ahead eliminates stress! So create a spreadsheet of the colleges you plan to visit. Include contact information on the sheet. Begin phoning in the early spring for summer interviews. There are only so many interview slots available, and they go fast. If the admissions office isn't yet scheduling when you call, put the date you can call back on your spreadsheet. Remember, spring is a good time to visit colleges, but it's also a good time for setting up interviews for the summer. Many colleges do not interview in the spring.

< 157 >

> Use the Internet to your advantage

In the "olden" days if you did not have the means to visit a school, you had no way to experience the campus. Many schools now offer virtual tours online as well as endless information about courses, professors, research opportunities, and other details. Once you've narrowed down your list of schools, use the Internet to explore each school in depth. Make sure to check out course offerings in departments that interest you, library facilities, social opportunities, campus landmarks, and any other areas of interest.

Take a virtual tour

< 158 >

> Don't arrive in a sweat after spending an hour driving in circles

Immediately after booking your appointment and writing the date in your spreadsheet, go online to mapquest.com and print out directions from your destination to the school. Then, in the folders you have neatly labeled for each college to which you are applying, include these directions. Better yet, ask the receptionist for directions and where to park—you don't want to arrive on time and then spend thirty minutes looking for a space.

Get directions

< 159 >

> Look for the right match

Many students overlook the basic fact that college is going to be their home for four years, so
take the time to make sure the college has everything you need. If you love engineering, don't
apply to a small liberal arts college that has no
engineering program. You'd be surprised how
many students just assume the college has
courses in their areas of interest when in fact
that's not the case. Plus, colleges will give extra
weight to applicants who prove they've done
their homework and know why a school is right
for them. You can never do enough research to
make sure you're picking schools that accommo-
date both your academic and your extracurricular interests.

the right match

< 160 >

> Get a handle on your temperament

Do you like a downshifted rhythm, or do you thrive when the pace is turned up? Match your temperament and learning styles with the college. Don't pick a college just because it might look good on a sticker plastered on your car's rear window. Maybe your heart sings by being out in nature. Hiking is your no-fail stress buster. Then pick a school that has access to the great outdoors. I love the Myers-Briggs test for the insight it can give us about how we function in the world. If your school offers this fun, non-graded, purely for self-knowledge test, by all means take it. The results may point you in an entirely different college direction.

Match your temperament

< 161 >

> Keep a detailed notebook of your impressions

After you visit a few colleges in a row, they may start to meld together. Suddenly you'll find yourself struggling to remember if it was Colby that had the beautiful water view or Colgate. Use the notes you take during visits on your applications by explaining what it was about the school that made you apply. The more specific you are about a professor you spoke with or a facility you visited, the better. Jot down names of major research facilities, library information, professors, and local eateries so when you get home, you'll remember every aspect of your visit.

Take notes

> Let go of "old associations"

When you arrive at a new campus, draw yourself a clean slate. Picture yourself at the school and write about how that might feel: in other words, consciously disregard the tales old Uncle Elwood told about fraternity bashes at College X and instead create your own impressions. Create for yourself a brief list of five things you loved about the campus and five things that bothered you. Later on you'll have time to compare your lists of pros and cons before committing to a particular school.

Draw a clean slate

< 163 >

> Visit classes

Even top colleges can have weak professors,
teaching assistants, and students with poor atti-
tudes in the classroom. The only way to find out
for sure is to observe a class during your visit.
Are the students jumping out of their chairs to
answer questions or falling asleep on their desks?
Is the professor holding their attention? Is it a
big lecture class or a small seminar? What is typ-
ical in that school? You'll learn a lot about a
school by attending classes during your visit.
Speak with professors: a big part of college is
devoted to sitting in classes and doing work, so
liking the professors will make a huge difference.
If you like English, stop by the department and
ask to speak to a professor so he or she can
describe what the department is like. You can
use this information later in your application
when you take a moment to explain why you
are applying to this school.

observe a class

< 164 >

> Follow your intuition or gut feelings

When you are visiting a college, plan an extra fifteen minutes to "go with your gut." Maybe your instinct tells you to seek out a particular professor or stop in the registrar's office and inquire about class sign-up procedures. Perhaps you want to find out more about the school's honor code or policy regarding summer school. After visiting classes, try to visualize yourself in that class—do you fit in? Would you be intimidated by your classmates, or did you feel they had your same academic zeal? Was the professor engaging, or did it feel as if the energy was just not there? Use the impressions to solidify your choices.

go with your gut

< 165 >

> Talk to students

It's one thing to like a college on paper after
reading a description, but it's another one
altogether to like the school after you've had a
chance to experience the campus firsthand and
talk to students. Ask them what they like best
about the school and what they'd change if they
had a chance. After speaking to students for ten
minutes on any campus, you'll be an expert on
what the college excels in and what it needs to
work on. Better to find out about problems
before you get there than after you arrive.

Talk to students

< 166 >

> Write down your mental notes

Let go of that old script that might tell you how "tough" the whole college process is, and instead affirm that "This is an enjoyable journey, an odyssey into my future, and I'm open to receiving input from a benevolent universe." Open your heart and watch for clues that come to you. For instance, you might hear the name of a college while listening to a radio program or read about a new study launched from a university department in just the field you're interested in. Jot these schools down on your list and follow up on the Internet for materials.

watch for clues

< 167 >

> Visit the areas on campus that coincide with your extracurricular interests

If the piano is important to you, make sure there are practice studios with time slots available for undergraduates. If you like to sing, check out the campus singing clubs to see if you'd fit in. Are you a workout fanatic? Go see what the gym is like. You will not be happy at a campus that does not meet your basic needs. Every student has special things that are important, so make sure you make your own personal list of important places to visit on campus.

Meet your basic needs

< 168 >

> Pick the best time to visit

Spring seems to be an ideal time to visit the colleges on your list. Just make sure not to visit during spring break. It's not a bad idea to visit on the weekends, as you can get a real feel for what weekend life is like on campus. Check with each college, however, as many don't schedule interviews until the summer months.

use the weekends

< 169 >

> Don't let your parents ruin your visit

When you go for your interview, it may make you less nervous to send your parents elsewhere, perhaps to listen to the information session. Parents tend to embarrass their children during interviews. Plus, the interviewer will see you as more mature if you are not dragging your parents in tow.

Leave your parents
behind

< 170 >

> Choose your travel partners carefully

Many students feel that their parents may sway them one way or another and prefer to make the college campus visits alone. Others don't want to worry about the logistics, so they seek their parents' input and are grateful that their parents will take the time to accompany them. Going with your best friend is rarely a good idea. This should be a trip to research and observe a college community, not an opportunity to hang out with friends from home.

A research trip

< 171 >

> Plan an overnight visit

Are the students studying on a Tuesday night, or
are they all out at parties? Though parties certainly have their place, you definitely want to
make sure you are at a college that provides a
healthy and safe learning environment, not one
that encourages students to develop lifelong
problems with drugs and alcohol.

overnight visit

< 172 >

> Stay sober

Yup, here's a nasty little truth—many high school students smoke their first joint, experience a wicked hangover, or spend an amorous evening with a stranger all on their overnight campus visits. Not good! Keep your values and morals intact, and don't join in the college debauchery— no matter how exciting it might seem. Not only could your behavior get back to the admissions office, but by compromising your values, you weaken your true self and move off center.

stay sober

< 173 >

> Just say no

Many times students will love a campus on paper, but find it less attractive during a visit. The truth is, the visit provides the more accurate picture, so if for some reason your dream school disappoints you, readjust your sights and don't narrow your list down to one school without visiting it and reaffirming your impressions.

readjust your sights

< 174 >

> Pay attention to first impressions

Your initial impressions offer you a lot. How does the campus "feel" to you? What sort of vibe do you pick up? Don't discount your feelings as unimportant. Think of them as a divining rod leading you to the right place. Sometimes decisions aren't just based on facts.

initial impressions offer a lot

< 175 >

Nine

Interviews

> Do They Matter?

You don't get ulcers from what you eat. You get them from what's eating you.
— Vicki Baum, novelist

> Learn some basic manners

Welcome to the real world—shake hands firmly with the interviewer; make eye contact (don't stare down at your lap); sit with your legs crossed or folded, not splayed open like you are on your couch eating pizza with your friends; and don't talk with your mouth full if you're at a coffee shop or restaurant. Don't hesitate to ask your interviewer questions as well about his or her experience at that college—remember, it's a two-way street, not an interrogation.

> Let Your Inner Light Shine

Few have strength of reason to overrule the perceptions of sense, and yet fewer have curiosity or benevolence to struggle long against the first impression: he who therefore fails to please in his salutation and address is at once rejected, and never obtains an opportunity of showing his latest excellences or essential qualities.

—Samuel Johnson

> Allow yourself to be in the moment

When you are in an interview, don't let yourself drift outside of your body so that you are merely an outside observer. Look into the interviewer's eyes, and connect with him or her in an authentic way. This is a great opportunity to let go and allow your true self to shine rather than forcing an image you think is the right one to present. You might try the following before heading behind those admissions officers' closed doors: Bring yourself fully to your present moment, observing the feel of the chair you are sitting on, the elements of the room you are in. Release thoughts of your past or future and just be in the moment.

INTERVIEWS

< 179 >

> Prepare a list of your key attributes

Outline your top two to four academic areas of interest and your top two to four extracurricular areas of interest. A thirty-minute interview won't allow enough time to touch on everything you've ever done, but you should be able to give examples of your principal strong points and interests. Thinking about them beforehand will give you an edge.

give examples

> Think back to a time when you felt successful

Can you recall a time in your life when you felt truly successful? What were you doing? Recall the feelings of being a success. What does it feel like? Carry that powerful feeling into your interview. Your confidence and feelings of success will immediately translate to the interviewer. Remember, it's okay to seem excited by what you do and the activities you are interested in— interviewers are looking for students who will lend a dynamic presence to the campus.

Think back

< 181 >

> Know what you're going to say no matter what they ask

Some interviewers ask very open-ended questions ("tell me about yourself"), while some ask you to list your courses, your teachers, your scores, and so on. If you've thought carefully about what makes you stand out academically and extracurricularly, it doesn't really matter what they ask—you'll be ready to fill in the details yourself, even if the question is just to describe yourself.

prepare yourself

< 182 >

> Bring appropriate written materials to help your interviewer

If you've prepared an activity list or an award list, feel free to bring it to the interview. Not all interviewers will want to see them, but some might. Just say something like, "If it would help you out, I brought a typed list of my extracurricular activities and my awards that I can leave with you." This phrasing gives the interviewer a way out if he or she doesn't want to see anything. Being fully prepared cuts the anxiety because you are in charge rather than feeling underprepared and reactive to what might occur.

Bring your lists

< 183 >

> Don't overdress or underdress

Overdressing indicates that you are trying to
compensate for a lack of real talent by showing
off your dress. Plus, you may be perceived as too
preppy or snobby if you wear *haut couture*.
Underdressing can be seen as a sign of disrespect.
Go for the middle of the road: boys can wear
chinos or pants other than jeans with any regular
shoe (as opposed to sneakers) with a button-
down shirt or polo (no tie necessary), while girls
can wear almost anything neat from a skirt and
blouse to pants and a sweater. Try to avoid any
extreme statements (nose rings, Mohawks,
spiked collars, tattoos, etc.).

Dress well

< 184 >

> Dress nicely but comfortably

If you aren't used to heels and are worried about tripping, don't wear them. The idea is to make yourself as comfortable as possible in an interview while putting the interviewer at ease as well. Never wear an outfit for the first time to an interview. You won't know if the skirt hikes up or if the pants are too long. Give your interview outfit a test run. It may sound funny, but don't forget to wear deodorant and go easy on the perfume or cologne. Leave a lasting impression with your presence not your smell.

Leave a lasting impression

< 185 >

> Don't be afraid to voice an opinion

If you think Clinton was a great president, say
so, but make sure you can back your opinions
with solid information. You wouldn't want to say
you thought the French deserved to be censured
for their lack of support in the war on Iraq
unless you were up on your current affairs.

voice an opinion

< 186 >

> Anxiety interferes with communication, and communicating is the goal of your college interviews

You want to find out from the interviewer the answers to all of your questions about his or her particular college. So relax, don't worry about yourself, and focus on the questions you'd like answered. Seek information rather than allowing those anxiety-powered neurotransmitters in your body to create static in your brief thirty- to forty-five-minute meeting.

focus on the questions

< 187 >

> Admit you don't know something rather than make up an answer

There are untold numbers of hilarious admissions stories about students who made up answers and were caught. Take our word for it— it's much better to say you don't know than to be caught in a lie or out of your field of knowledge.

Don't make up an answer

< 188 >

> Don't focus on your fears

Focusing on your fears or visualizing dreaded outcomes can manifest just what you don't want. Instead, each time your mind drifts to picturing a negative outcome, erase the blackboard of your mind or put a red slash through the mental picture. Now, picture what you'd like to occur—how you see the interview unfolding.

picture what you'd like to occur

< 189 >

> Prepare a list of questions

Almost every interviewer will begin or end the interview by asking if you have any questions about the school. Rather than trying to improvise, write out a list of well-thought-out questions and bring them with you. Don't just ask questions that you could look up on a Web site; rather, ask questions that show you really care about what life on campus is like. Skim the campus newspaper before the interview to see if there are any controversies brewing and ask what the campus is doing to address these concerns.

ask questions that
show you care

< 190 >

> Ask for a business card

It's polite to send a handwritten thank-you note
(not an e-mail in this case), since your interviewer took time out of the day to speak to you.
It helps to mention one thing that came up in the
interview so that he or she remembers who you
are: "I really enjoyed speaking to you about the
new science facility on your campus." Oftentimes interviewers will go out of their way to
push for you in the admissions process if they
sense a real connection has been established.

Handwrite a
thank-you note

< 191 >

> Don't let yourself get flustered

Occasionally interviewers ask really off-base questions about something you have no idea about. It's better to laugh it off and say, "Gosh, I'm embarrassed to admit this, but I've been so swamped by my homework this month that I've fallen behind in my current events. I haven't had a chance to read about the crisis in Darfur yet."

laugh it off

< 192 >

> Come up with a mantra

When you are nervous or disoriented, silently repeating a word can shift your state of mind completely. Come up with a word or phrase to keep you calm before your interview. "Peaceful me" or "Steady" might help.

keep calm

< 193 >

> Don't wait for a question

If there's something you are dying to talk about
and the interviewer doesn't ask you about it, feel
free to interject at any time: "I also wanted to
mention my martial arts training, which takes up
ten to fifteen hours per week."

feel free to interject

< 194 >

> Speak concisely

When you have answered a question, without saying "like" or "um," then end it. Don't babble on just to fill the space with sound. You might practice the week before you head off for an interview by being mindful of any lazy speech habits. Ask your friends to let you know when you slip.

speak concisely

> Don't try to judge how the interview is going

I spent years doing interviews, and the funniest part was that some students who truly had horrible interviews left feeling they did a great job (because our job is to make them feel comfortable and to market the school), while other very competitive students who actually did great for some reason felt they fell short. Don't try to second-guess how the interview went. It's healthier to just move on.

Don't try to
second-guess

< 196 >

> Remain positive

There's nothing that brings down the energy of
an interview faster than negative talk. Keep
your tone positive about any subject you are
discussing. Leave words and phrases such as
"difficult" and "I could have, but . . ." out of the
conversation. Don't "diss" another school or
make excuses for yourself.

Remain positive

< 197 >

Ten

And Then There Is . . . General Tips for the High School Years

> Be a Type-A Planner

I've had many troubles in my life but the worst of them never came.

—James A. Garfield

> Keep a day planner that you can carry with you to all of your classes

Don't just keep track of nightly homework, but also keep track of longer projects, papers, labs, and so on. That way you will be able to budget your time better, use weekends more effectively, and have time to just hang out and be a teenager every once in a while. Being a good student does not mean you're not entitled to have a life.

> Weave the Following into Your Daily Life

Keep your sense of humor. There's enough stress in the rest of your life to let bad shots ruin a game you're supposed to enjoy.
—Amy Strum Alcott, U.S. golfer

> Just because you're applying to college doesn't mean your daily rituals have to stop

Most families have developed rituals and traditions over the years. Family dinners, for instance, are a wonderful time to "center down" with your family. It's tempting when you're busy to grab a slice of pizza on the run and catch up with your family later, but figure out a way to sit down and actually give thanks for your food, taste what you are eating, and bring yourself to the present moment. In the long run, this halt to the frenetic activity of your life and sticking with a simple ritual pays big rewards in terms of a less stress-packed life. Studies show that kids who eat with their family at least three times a week have better academic performance than those who rarely eat with their family.

< 201 >

> Look forward

During your freshman or sophomore year, buy a Fiske or Peterson's guide to colleges and start to browse through to get an idea of what type of college you will be interested in. By making a preliminary list, you can start to map out possible campus visits at least to those that may be a few hours' driving distance away. As discussed earlier, don't wait until junior year. Planning ahead will also direct your efforts in school toward doing better and staying focused if you have a final goal in mind.

start to browse early

< 202 >

> You are in charge of your life

Every moment you are free to make a choice.
Study for the chemistry test or don't. Become
organized and start the college search junior year
or not. Hang posters for your pet-walking business or just hope you'll be called. The more you
acknowledge the truth that you are responsible
for the life you experience, the more independent
you will become. You are living the life today
that you planned last year. If you are vague
with your choices, your results will be just as
lackluster.

You get to choose

< 203 >

> Request information early on

Once you take the PSAT you will be put on the mailing lists for many colleges. However, before junior fall it's worth it to take some time to either call your favorite ten colleges or request the information online in order to be added to their mailing lists. That way you won't have to worry about obtaining applications at the last minute (not all colleges have them online), and you'll be able to start reading about each school to see which one is right for you.

call your favorite ten colleges

< 204 >

> Applaud yourself for the kindness you show others, not just your achievements

The truth is, pushing harder and racking up achievements and accolades can be accomplished by anyone with enough caffeine and fortitude. But the person who is genuinely kind to others magnetizes that goodwill right back into their lives. Balance kindness with a focus on your own path. Give from your heart and watch the bounty show up in your life. The truth is, kindness does count!

Give from your heart

< 205 >

> Stay ahead

Make it a point to stay a week ahead in your classes. Good students use holidays and vacations to catch up on class work and get ahead. You'll notice the difference especially in complex classes like advanced science and math if you read ahead in the textbook. When your teacher suddenly covers a topic in class, for you it will be more like a review than hearing it for the first time. Even if you don't understand everything the first time you read it, you can fill in the gaps when your teacher covers the material.

stay ahead

< 206 >

> Banish fear

Fear can be one of the biggest obstacles you face as you move toward the college admissions process. Shift from fear to trust and come up with a mental trigger—a switch to flip—when you are entering the doubt zone. Once this switch is flipped, you move to trusting your guidance, yourself, and your path. No person, situation, or thing can take your good from you. You are exactly where you are meant to be and all is well. Picture that big red switch. Feeling anxious and fearful? Close your eyes and flip the switch to trust, faith, and calm.

shift from fear to trust

< 207 >

> Use study halls and any free time during the day wisely

You can cut down dramatically on the amount of homework you have in the evening if you take advantage of free periods, lunch hours, and time after school before clubs or sports start up. If you are an athlete, you'll be away at games or busy at practice until late at night, so it's a good idea to use time during the school day to stay ahead and get a jump on homework. Be sure to use weekends to get ahead as well if you know you have a tough week of away games, or events that require travel time. Bring work with you on public transportation like buses and cars to chip away at homework.

chip away at homework

< 208 >

> Source yourself throughout your day

You have an ever-present opportunity to renew yourself, without withdrawing from the world. It's as simple as pausing in the midst of your day and taking a deep breath, imagining it is filling your body with strength, energy, and positive light. You can do this as you walk between classes, wait in the lunch line, or sit on the bench of the playing field. Create little habits of calm throughout your busy day. When you hear the annoying "ding, ding, ding" of car keys in the ignition, for instance, use it as a reminder to take a deep breath, drop your shoulders, and relax.

Create little habits of calm

< 209 >

> Stop to evaluate

Are you unhappy about how any of your activities are going? Any of your classes? Don't be miserable if you don't have to. You can change a class, drop an activity, or start a new activity. Remember, colleges want to see you do something you love, not something you are forced to do. This doesn't give you license to drop out of a difficult class at the first sign of trouble, but it does mean you should take the time to speak to a teacher to help get you back on track if necessary.

Don't be miserable if you don't have to

< 210 >

> Let go of any past mistakes you've made

If you make a mistake, forgive yourself and move forward. Then, think about how you want to approach school or activities differently this year than you have in the past. Create a clear picture in your mind. Write down the qualities you'd like to have more of: organization, understanding, joy, appreciation, acceptance. Keep the list handy to remind yourself of the picture you imagined.

forgive yourself and move forward

< 211 >

> **Be confident and secure**

High school students spend too much of their time feeling they are "losing" in the competition. Change your attitude. You can correct a bad situation. Who said being a good student and leader was easy? Even the brightest, most confident students have moments of doubt—relax, it's normal!

You can correct a bad situation

< 212 >

> Remember, everything changes, especially during this time in your life

Rather than fear change, embrace it and trust that you are moving down your life path full of divine guidance and support.

Embrace change

< 213 >

> Keep your expectations realistic

Are your parents trying to force you to go to
their alma mater? Don't let this happen! You can
push yourself hard, but there is a limit to your
achievement level relative to your abilities. If you
have all mid-600 scores on SAT I's and II's, it's
not likely you'll go to Harvard, nor should you.
Choose schools where you'd feel comfortable
and challenged, but not overwhelmed.

comfortable and challenged

< 214 >

> Give thanks

There's a wonderful anonymous saying that reads, "For that which you are thankful you will never be denied." Make sure to develop an attitude of gratitude for all the good in your life. It's easy to get off track when you are so busy thinking of the future. Create a habit of listing a few things you are thankful for at each day's end, and notice how this magical elixir colors your outlook.

develop an attitude of gratitude

< 215 >

> Use any tip factors to your advantage

Are you a legacy? Recruited athlete? Strong minority student? Typically the top colleges fill almost 40 percent of their class with special applicants. Don't neglect to mention on the application that your mother or father attended that school—as long as there are preferences in the admissions process, take advantage of them.

take advantage of preferences

< 216 >

> Keep your own counsel

Once you hit the fall semester of your senior year, it might seem that all anyone can talk about is college. The level of stress escalates after these conversations. "I'm applying to Stanford and the cross-country coach has contacted me," or "Did you hear that Sam's dad went to Colby as did his dad and his dad . . . and there's a science building at the school with their name," or "WHAT, you haven't taken SAT prep?" Keeping your own counsel helps you remain out of the contagious chatter than can push your anxiety buttons. Take a deep breath and excuse yourself when this talk begins. Then, remind yourself of your clear list of action items and what you have already accomplished. You are just fine! Besides, a lot of the talk is myth anyway.

Keep your own
counsel

< 217 >

> Enlist your parents as allies

Parents want to help, so give them things they can do that will keep them involved without taking over the process. For example, your parents can stamp and self-address the envelopes for your teacher recommendations so they can feel part of the process and save you time. Don't order them to do things, but if they want to get involved, it is easy to give them work that complements the work you are doing.

Parents want to help

< 218 >

> Include your parents

Parents can be wonderful resources during this
time. Obviously you shouldn't have them write
your essays for you, but do ask for their advice
and see them as partners rather than obstacles in
your college admissions process.

Parents can be
wonderful resources

< 219 >

Resources for Your Admissions Journey

> Web sites

www.collegeboard.com

This site is full to the brim with great resources for your college search. Our favorite is the college comparison feature. Go to College Quick Finder on the site and you can see your favorite school's statistics listed side by side.

www.collegeconfidential.com

We love the bulletin boards that allow people to chat about admission practices at all the top colleges—join in the conversations!

www.dontworrygetin.com

This is the companion site to the book you are holding in your hand! We'll give you updated

< 221 >

information, resources, and even thoughts for
the day to keep you motivated and stress free.

www.fastweb.com

One of the Web's best sites for scholarship
information.

www.hernandezcollegeconsulting.com

Michele's Web site, which has many useful statistics on Ivy League schools, a free newsletter full
of pertinent reminders and tips, and the all-
important Academic Index Calculator.

www.jhu.edu

The Johns Hopkins Web site that has links for the
major talent searches in the country, including
the Duke TIP program and many others.

www.meditationcenter.com

Ahhhhh . . . take up meditation during your college

< 222 >

application years and not only will it make the process less stressful, but may become a lifelong habit!

www.spiritualparenting.com

Mimi's Web site, which has tons of great information as well as a terrific free newsletter.

> Admission and College-Specific Books

Compiled and edited by the staff of the *Yale Daily News* **The Insider's Guide to the Colleges: Students on Campus Tell You What You Really Want to Know.** St. Martin's Griffin, New York, 2004.

Contains juicy student-written descriptions of what life at each college is really like.

College Prowler Guidebooks series (written by various authors)

Students continue to tell us that this collection of college specific books—reviewing 200 colleges—gives them the real inside knowledge they can't get

< 223 >

from a visit or college catalog. Their Web site www.collegeprowler.com sells the books directly.

The Princeton Review. The Best 351 Colleges, 2005 edition. Princeton: 2004.

A helpful summary of key facts and figures for the nation's top colleges.

Avery, Christopher, et al. ***The Early Admissions Game: Joining the Elite.*** Cambridge, Harvard University Press: 2003.

A must-read for those who want real numbers on the early admissions process based on a study the authors did over several years. We couldn't put it down.

Bauld, Harry. ***On Writing the College Application Essay: The Key to Acceptance and the College of Your Choice.*** San Francisco, Harper Resource: 1987.

This is one of our favorite books on the college application essay, written by Michele's friend and former colleague Harry Bauld. Highly recommended both for its superb content and humor.

Fiske, Edward. *Fiske Guide to Colleges 2005*. New York, Sourcebooks: 2004.

A good all-around guide to colleges with helpful thumbnail descriptions.

Hernandez, Michele. *A is for Admission*. New York, Warner Books: 1999.

Michele's first book, which explains in great detail the academic index, the inside story on standardized testing, and a firsthand view of the Ivy League admissions process.

Hernandez, Michele. *Acing the College Application.* New York, Ballantine Books: 2002.

Michele's book that focuses on the application itself.

Hughes, Chuck. *What It Really Takes to Get Into Ivy League and Other Highly Selective Colleges*. New York, McGraw-Hill: 2003.

Written by a senior admissions officer at Harvard, this book is one of the few that delivers what it promises.

< 225 >

Pope, Loren. *Colleges That Change Lives: 40 Schools You Should Know About Even If You're Not a Straight-A Student*. New York, Penguin Books: 2000.

Pope is directly responsible for popularizing some great colleges that used to get overlooked—but not anymore. Many have become hot schools!

Pope, Loren. *Looking Beyond the Ivy League: Finding the College That's Right for You*. New York, Penguin Books: 1996.

Again, Pope's voice is refreshing as he guides students to what is really important: a thoughtful college match.

> Other great reads

Carlson, Richard, Ph.D. *Don't Sweat the Small Stuff for Teens: Simple Ways to Keep Your Cool in Stressful Times*. New York: Hyperion, 2000.

Read this little book to help keep things in perspective.

< 226 >

Covey, Sean. *The 7 Habits of Highly Effective Teens: The Ultimate Teenage Success Guide.* New York: Simon & Schuster, 1998.

If you garner even one helpful tip from this book, it's worth the purchase price.

Frankl, Viktor. *Man's Search for Meaning.* Washington Square Press, 1997.

Here's a not-so-light read that will remind you what's really important in life.

Kushner, Harold. *When Bad Things Happen to Good People.* Avon, 1983.

Yup, bad things do seem to happen, but this book helps us get a grip.

Peyser, Randy. *Crappy to Happy: Small Steps to Big Happiness NOW!.* Boston, MA:Red Wheel/Weiser, 2002.

The title says it all.

> Tutoring

Our top tips for selecting a tutor include:

1. Figure out exactly why you need a tutor. Do you need to relearn material that you never fully understood or prepare for specific tests? Once you articulate exactly what it is you want from a tutor, you can better begin the process of finding one who works for you.

2. Ask for references from parents and students.

3. Ask if the tutor has any concrete results or statistics such as test scores improving or students moving to a higher level of a subject.

4. Make sure to identify the tutor's experience working one-on-one with students.

5. Start with a provisional agreement so you can make sure you are a good match.

< 228 >

> Summer Programs

Here's a list of our favorite competitive precollege programs. You can find more info on the Web, of course, in terms of dates, applications, and specific subject focus.

Brown University
Carnegie Mellon University
Columbia University
Cornell University
Dartmouth College (Rassias ten-day language immersion programs and Dartmouth Debate Institute)
Dickinson College
Duke University (and the special Talent Identification Program—TIP)
Georgetown University
Harvard University
John Hopkins University (and Center for Talented Youth—CTY program)
Northwestern University
Skidmore College
Stanford University
Tufts University
University of California at Berkeley
University of Pennsylvania
Yale University

< 229 >

RESOURCES

>Acknowledgments

We would like to acknowledge and thank the many wonderful families and teenagers with whom we have worked.

Michele: Talking almost daily with Mimi, the parenting guru, has changed how I perceive my day-to-day life—her influence is like a double shot of espresso plus a pep talk all in one. I am so glad we met through this project and have become fast friends. Of course I would like to thank my wonderful and supportive husband, Bruce; daughter, Alexia; and baby son, Ian, who provide all the joy and excitement anyone could ask for (and then some). Add to the mix our two golden retrievers, Harris and Bree, and it's a full-time party. Finally, my parents, Cynthia and Hank, and my sister, Jennifer, have always been a source of inspiration, as have all my terrific friends over the years.

Mimi: It's great fun to work with admissions guru Michele A. Hernandez, whose energy cannot be matched. I would also like to thank my husband, Tom, and daughters, Whitney and Elizabeth, who inspire and delight me every day! And to the wonderful teachers my daughters have been privileged to learn from over the years, I am grateful to you all.

< 230 >